The Elephant in the Sanctuary

Comparing

the Republican Platform to the Bible

James R. King

7/25/2020

Forward written by Dr. Gary Jarnagin

Dr. Jarnagin is an Associate Professor of the

Balthasar Hubmaier School of Theology and

Missions at Truett McConnell University in

Cleveland, GA.

Forward

The work presented is a snippet of biblical responses to the worldly attacks and ever-present challenges which face the Church in today's culture wars. James King has introduced and addressed selected cultural battles through the only spiritual and moral compass that exists for a follower of Christ, The

Bible. The reader of this work will

enjoy the biblical responses to these

cultural enemies of sound biblical

doctrine. After absorbing these

important doctrinal messages

addressed in this work, the follower of

Christ should be motivated to pursue

a deeper understanding of these topics

and many more which invade the

Church today. While the biblical

compass should always be the last

source of authority for anyone

desiring to follow the will of God, this

introduction to the ongoing apostasy of the age is a great place to start for defending the faith.

Thesis

Churches today are abandoning traditional views and practices to embrace more worldly ideals. Denominations, such as certain branches of the Episcopalians, have openly embraced homosexuality, transgenderism, and many other Leftist idealogues. The worldly push within many denominations is at such odds with the traditional beliefs of the Church, that many denominations, such as the Methodists and even the once ultra-Conservative Southern Baptist Convention, seem to be in danger of fracturing. As the culture war intensifies within the Church, I feel as though there are questions which need to be asked of each individual who professes to be a Christian, namely how each social issue dividing our nation- and now the Church- relates to the Bible itself.

As is often repeated throughout the Scriptures, a house built upon sand will collapse while a house built upon solid ground will weather many storms. The foundation for Christians must be the Bible, as it is the very bedrock upon which Christianity has flourished and spread. Additionally, many verses in Scripture, such as 2 Timothy 3:16, inform Christians that the Bible is literally the Word of God and is therefore inerrant and unchanging. While it is true many verses can be argued to be interpretive, if Christians hold a

Biblical worldview, and all Christians should, then we have a theological necessity to allow the Bible to shape how we view and respond to all aspects of life, including social and political issues.

For the purpose of this paper, my goal is not to persuade the reader to become a Conservative, but rather, to provide Bible verses which directly relate to each societal or political issue addressed within this paper. With each issue, I present my own conclusion, but I intentionally present each topic in a manner in which the reader should draw his or her own conclusion about each issue. Again, the purpose for writing this is to persuade the Church as a whole to reexamine many issues certain denominations have taken up, and to urge denominations to reconcile what is Godly against the influences of the world that have been allowed to thrive within those denominations.

The Biblical Role of Government

Before I begin to examine social and political issues, I believe it is important to first examine the role of governments as outlined in the Scriptures. Romans 13:1-2 clearly shows that every ruling authority that exists has been established by God. That means the authority of man is derived from God. Additionally, those in government positions are described as servants of God in Romans 13:4 and Romans 13:6. We also learn through John 19:10-11, Psalms 75:7, and Daniel 2:21 that the authority God gives governments can also be removed by God.

In Romans 13:4, we see governments are created to serve as dispensers of Earthly justice. In verses such as Deuteronomy 32:32 and Romans 12:19, we see that full justice and vengeance are God's alone to enact, but we also see in Romans 13:4 that governments are ordained to "bear the sword" and thus carry out Earthly justice against the wrong. In fact, Romans 13:4 has often been interpreted to justify the waging of wars, something made additionally clear in 1 Peter 2:14, which outlines waging wars in defense against those who do evil (another responsibility of government). Furthermore, since governments are ordained by God and Christians are to be "fishers of men"

(Matthew 4:19), it is only right for Christians to seek to influence governments as a means of shaping the society around us by taking Biblical stands on the issues outlined throughout this paper.

Now that we have discussed the Biblical roles of government, in the pages that follow we will examine how Christians should respond to social and political issues in a Biblical manner.

Love

It seems as though a growing misconception, especially among young people, is that love means anything pleasing under the sun. Yet, the Septuagint, which was the New Testament as originally written in Greek, specifically lists three, arguably four (I will define all four), words in Greek that all mean *love* in our English language- eros, philia, storgi, and agape. Eros is a word that, in essence, means lust (it is where we obtain the word erotic from). Philia means "brotherly love" (philia is actually where we get Philadelphia from- "Philadelphia" means city of brotherly love). Storgi means family love. Agape means Godly and unconditional love. It is important to note, some Biblical scholars consider the word Storgi to be interchangeable with Philia, and thus some Greek teachers will only teach eros, philia, and agape.

Regardless of which specific Greek words for love appear within the Septuagint, I believe it is foremost important we define what love really is. In doing so, I believe all Christians will be able to better understand why some social or political issues may be perceived as good, when in fact, they are sinful. To fully understand what love is, I believe we need to first examine what Scripture specifically says about love. The following verses speak directly about love, and should therefore form the basis of the response of the Church to this societal issue.

- 1 Corinthians 13:4-5 reads, "Love is patient, love is kind. It does not envy, it does not boast, it is not proud. It does not dishonor others, it is not self-seeking, it is not easily angered, it keeps no record of wrongs."

- Colossians 3:14 says, "And over all these virtues put on

love, which binds them all together in perfect unity."

- 1 John 4:15 reads, "And so we know and rely on the love God has for us. God is love. Whoever lives in love lives in God, and God in them."

- Ephesians 4:2 says, "Be completely humble and gentle; be patient, bearing with one another in love."

- Romans 12:9 reads, "Love must be sincere. Hate what is evil; cling to what is good."

- John 15:12 says, "My command is this: Love each other as I have loved you."

- 1 John 4:20 reads, "Whoever claims to love God yet hates a brother or sister is a liar. For whoever does not love their brother and sister, whom they have seen, cannot love God, whom they have not seen."

- John 15:13 says, "Greater love has no one than this: to lay down one's life for one's friends."

- 1 John 4:18 reads, "There is no fear in love. But perfect love drives out fear, because fear has to do with punishment. The one who fears is not made perfect in love."

- 1 John 4:8 says, "Whoever does not love does not know God, because God is love."

- Proverbs 10:12 reads, "Hatred stirs up conflict, but love covers over all wrongs."

Considering these verses, I do not believe it is possible to have love without discipline. I also do not believe actual love can be manifested with selfishness. Furthermore, if God is love (and, according to Scripture, He is), then what is sinful can not truly be love. After all, sin is the absence of, or rebellion against, God.

Abortion

In 1973, the United States Supreme Court provided a ruling in the case of *Roe VS Wade* which legalized abortion throughout the United States. In the years following, many churches have openly embraced, and even advocated for, abortion. In May of 2019, female minister Jes Kast, of the United Church of Christ, made national headlines when she decried the pro-life legislation enacted by many States around the same time. To examine how the Church should respond to abortion, we must first consider what the Bible says about the issue. The following verses speak directly about abortion, and should therefore form the basis of the response of the Church to this societal issue.

- Exodus 20:13 says, "You shall not murder".

- Psalm 139:13-16 says, "For you created my inmost being; you knit me together in my mother's womb. I praise you because I am fearfully and wonderfully made; your works are wonderful, I know that full well. My frame was not hidden from you when I was made in the secret place, when I was woven together in the depths of the earth. Your eyes saw my unformed body; all the days ordained for me were written in your book before one of them came to be."

- Jeremiah 1:5 reads, "Before I formed you in the womb, I knew you, before you were born, I set you apart; I appointed you as a prophet to the nations."

- Psalm 127: 3 says, "Children are a heritage from the Lord, offspring a reward from Him."

- Proverbs 6:16-19 reads, "There are six things the Lord hates, seven that are detestable to him: haughty eyes, a lying tongue, hands that shed innocent blood, a heart that devises wicked schemes, feet that are quick to rush into evil, a false witness who pours out lies, and a person who stirs up conflict in the community."

Considering these verses, I do not believe one can hold a Biblical worldview and not recognize each child, even in the womb, was created by God, is unique, and that, therefore, abortion is no less than murder.

Homosexuality

In 2015, the United States Supreme Court provided a ruling in the case of *Obgerfeller VS Hodges* which legalized same-sex "marriage" throughout the United States. In the years prior to and following the ruling of *Obgerfeller*, many churches have openly embraced, and even advocated for, LGBTQ+ issues. Denominations, such as Liberal congregations within the Episcopalian Church, have ordained gay, lesbian, and even transgender clergy, and have also performed same-sex "wedding" ceremonies. More recently to the time of this paper's publishing, the Methodist Church is at a breaking point on the issue of homosexuality and other LGBTQ+ issues. To examine how the Church should respond to homosexuality, we must first consider what the Bible says about the issue. The following verses speak directly about homosexuality, and should therefore form the basis of the response of the Church to this societal issue.

- Genesis 19:1-11 reads, "That evening the two angels came to the entrance of the city of Sodom. Lot was sitting there, and when he saw them, he stood up to meet them. Then he welcomed them and bowed with his face to the ground. "My lords," he said, "come to my home to wash your feet,

and be my guests for the night.

You may then get up early in

the morning and be on your

way again." "Oh no," they

replied. "We'll just spend the

night out here in the city

square." But Lot insisted, so at

last they went home with him.

Lot prepared a feast for them,

complete with fresh bread made

without yeast, and they ate. But

before they retired for the night,

all the men of Sodom, young

and old, came from all over the

city and surrounded the house.

They shouted to Lot, "Where

are the men who came to spend

the night with you? Bring them

out to us so we can have sex

with them!" So Lot stepped

outside to talk to them, shutting

the door behind him. "Please,

my brothers," he begged, "don't

do such a wicked thing. Look, I

have two virgin daughters. Let

me bring them out to you, and you can do with them as you wish. But please, leave these men alone, for they are my guests and are under my protection." "Stand back!" they shouted. "This fellow came to town as an outsider, and now he's acting like our judge! We'll treat you far worse than those other men!" And they lunged toward Lot to break down the door. But the two angels reached out, pulled Lot into the house, and bolted the door. Then they blinded all the men, young and old, who were at the door of the house, so they gave up trying to get inside."

- Leviticus 18:22 says, "Do not practice homosexuality, having sex with another man as with a woman. It is a detestable sin." (NLT)

- Leviticus 20:13 reads, "If a man practices homosexuality,

having sex with another man as with a woman, both men have committed a detestable act. They must both be put to death, for they are guilty of a capital offense." (NLT)

- Judges 19:16-24 says, "That evening an old man came home from his work in the fields. He was from the hill country of Ephraim, but he was living in Gibeah, where the people were from the tribe of Benjamin.

When he saw the travelers

sitting in the town square, he

asked them where they were

from and where they were

going. "We have been in

Bethlehem in Judah," the man

replied. "We are on our way to

a remote area in the hill country

of Ephraim, which is my home.

I traveled to Bethlehem, and

now I'm returning home. But no

one has taken us in for the

night, even though we have

everything we need. We have straw and feed for our donkeys and plenty of bread and wine for ourselves." "You are welcome to stay with me," the old man said. "I will give you anything you might need. But whatever you do, don't spend the night in the square." So he took them home with him and fed the donkeys. After they washed their feet, they ate and drank together. While they were enjoying themselves, a crowd of troublemakers from the town surrounded the house. They began beating at the door and shouting to the old man, "Bring out the man who is staying with you so we can have sex with him." The old man stepped outside to talk to them. "No, my brothers, don't do such an evil thing. For this man is a guest in my house, and such a thing would be shameful. Here, take my virgin daughter and this man's concubine. I will bring them out to you, and you can abuse them and do whatever you like. But don't do such a shameful thing to this man."

- 1 Kings 14:24 reads, "And there were also male cult prostitutes in the land. They did according to all the abominations of the nations that the LORD drove out before the people of Israel."

- 1 Kings 15:12 says, "He put away the male cult prostitutes out of the land and removed all the idols that his fathers had made."

- 2 Kings 23:7 reads, "He also tore down the living quarters of the male and female shrine prostitutes that were inside the Temple of the LORD, where the women wove coverings for the Asherah pole."

- Romans 1:18-32 says, "But God shows his anger from heaven against all sinful, wicked people who suppress the truth by their wickedness.... Yes, they knew God, but they wouldn't worship him as God or even give him thanks. And they began to think up foolish ideas of what God was like. As a result, their minds became dark and confused. Claiming to

be wise, they instead became

utter fools. And instead of

worshiping the glorious, ever-

living God, they worshiped

idols made to look like mere

people and birds and animals

and reptiles. So God abandoned

them to do whatever shameful

things their hearts desired. As a

result, they did vile and

degrading things with each

other's bodies. They traded the

truth about God for a lie. So they worshiped and served the things God created instead of the Creator himself, who is worthy of eternal praise! Amen. That is why God abandoned them to their shameful desires. Even the women turned against the natural way to have sex and instead indulged in sex with each other. And the men, instead of having normal sexual relations with women, burned with lust for each other. Men

did shameful things with other

men, and as a result of this sin,

they suffered within themselves

the penalty they deserved.

Since they thought it foolish to

acknowledge God, he

abandoned them to their foolish

thinking and let them do things

that should never be done.

Their lives became full of every

kind of wickedness, sin, greed,

hate, envy, murder, quarreling,

deception, malicious behavior, and gossip. They are backstabbers, haters of God, insolent, proud, and boastful. They invent new ways of sinning, and they disobey their parents. They refuse to understand, break their promises, are heartless, and have no mercy. They know God's justice requires that those who do these things deserve to die, yet they do them anyway.

Worse yet, they encourage others to do them, too."

- 1 Corinthians 6:9-11 reads, "Don't you realize that those who do wrong will not inherit the Kingdom of God? Don't fool yourselves. Those who indulge in sexual sin, or who worship idols, or commit adultery, or are male prostitutes, or practice homosexuality, or are thieves, or greedy people, or drunkards, or are abusive, or cheat peoplenone of these will inherit the Kingdom of God. Some of you were once like that. But you were cleansed; you were made holy; you were made right with God by calling on the name of the Lord Jesus Christ and by the Spirit of our God."

- 1 Timothy 1:8-10 says, "Now we know that the law is good, if one uses it lawfully, understanding this, that the law is not laid down for the just but for the lawless and disobedient, for the ungodly and sinners, for the unholy and profane, for those who strike their fathers and mothers, for murderers, the sexually immoral, men who practice homosexuality, enslavers, liars, perjurers, and whatever else is contrary to sound doctrine"

- Jude 7 reads, "And don't forget Sodom and Gomorrah and their neighboring towns, which were filled with immorality and every kind of sexual perversion. Those cities were destroyed by fire and serve as a warning of the eternal fire of God's judgment."

- Matthew 19:4-6 says, "Haven't you read," he replied, "that at the beginning the Creator 'made them male and female,' and said, 'For this reason a man will leave his father and mother and be united to his wife, and the two will become one flesh? So they are no longer two, but one flesh. Therefore what God has joined together, let no one separate."

Considering these verses, I do not believe it is possible to hold a Biblical worldview and support homosexuality.

Transgenderism

In 2015, the United States Supreme Court provided a ruling in the case of *Obgerfeller VS Hodges* which legalized same-sex "marriage" throughout the United States, and in the years following LGBTQ+ advocacy groups have become increasingly vocal. In the years prior and following the ruling of *Obgerfeller*, many churches have openly embraced, and even advocated for, LGBTQ+ issues. Denominations, such as the Episcopalian Church, have ordained gay, lesbian, transgender, and even "cisgender" and "non-gender conforming" clergy. More recently to the time of this paper's publishing, the Methodist Church is at a breaking point on the issue of homosexuality and other LGBTQ+ issues. To examine how the Church should respond to transgenderism, we must first consider what the Bible says about the issue. The following verses speak directly about human genders, and should therefore form the basis of the response of the Church to this societal issue.

- Genesis 1:27 reads, "So God created mankind in his own image, in the image of God he created them, male and female he created them."

- Matthew 19:4-9 reads,

  "Haven't you read," he replied,

  "that at the beginning the

Creator 'made them male and female,' and said, 'For this reason a man will leave his father and mother and be united to his wife, and the two will become one flesh? So they are no longer two, but one flesh. Therefore what God has joined together, let no one separate."

"Why then," they asked, "did Moses command that a man give his wife a certificate of divorce and send her away?"

Jesus replied, "Moses permitted you to divorce your wives because your hearts were hard. But it was not this way from the beginning. I tell you that anyone who divorces his wife, except for sexual immorality, and marries another woman commits adultery."

- Psalm 139:13-14 says, "For you created my inmost being; you knit me together in my mother's womb. I praise you because I am fearfully and wonderfully made; your works are wonderful, I know that full well."

Considering these verses, I do not believe it is possible to have a Biblical worldview and believe we can be any gender other than what we were born as.

Egalitarianism

For many years, denominations such as the Liberal branches of the Presbyterian Church, have ordained female pastors. Other churches have vocally advocated for the theorized gender wage gap, and some churches have even sought to place women above men. Recently, a Christian theological college began teaching it's students that God is feminine and even cisgender. To examine how the

Church should respond to feminism, we must first consider what the Bible says about the issue. The following verses speak directly about feminism, and should therefore form the basis of the response of the Church to this societal issue.

- 1 Corinthians 11:12 says, "For as woman was made from man, so man is now born of woman. And all things are from God."

- Genesis 2:18 reads, "Then the Lord God said, "It is not good that the man should be alone; I will make him a helper fit for him."

- 1 Corinthians 7:1-40 says, "Now concerning the matters about which you wrote: "It is good for a man not to have sexual relations with a woman." But because of the temptation to sexual immorality, each man should have his own wife and each woman her own husband. The husband should give to his wife her conjugal rights, and likewise the wife to her husband. For the wife does not have authority over her own body, but the husband does. Likewise the husband does not have authority over his own body, but the wife does. Do not deprive one another, except perhaps by agreement for a limited time, that you may devote yourselves to prayer; but then come together again, so that Satan may not tempt you because of your lack of self-control."

- Titus 2:1-5 reads, "But as for you, teach what accords with sound doctrine. Older men are to be sober-minded, dignified, self-controlled, sound in faith, in love, and in steadfastness. Older women likewise are to be reverent in behavior, not slanderers or slaves to much wine. They are to teach what is good, and so train the young women to love their husbands and children, to be self-controlled, pure, working at home, kind, and submissive to their own husbands, that the word of God may not be reviled."

- 1 Peter 3:1-22 says, "Likewise, wives, be subject to your own husbands, so that even if some

do not obey the word, they may

be won without a word by the

conduct of their wives, when

they see your respectful and

pure conduct. Do not let your

adorning be external—the

braiding of hair and the putting

on of gold jewelry, or the

clothing you wear— but let

your adorning be the hidden

person of the heart with the

imperishable beauty of a gentle

and quiet spirit, which in God's sight is very precious. For this is how the holy women who hoped in God used to adorn themselves, by submitting to their own husbands."

- 1 Timothy 2:12 reads, "But I do not allow a woman to teach or exercise authority over a man, but to remain quiet."

Considering these verses, I do not believe it is possible to hold a

Biblical worldview and believe that

women are allowed by God to serve

as pastors, are superior to men (or that

men are superior to women), or that

both genders can do fully what the

other can.

Government Welfare Programs

On social media and other public forums, many Christians will argue government welfare programs should be supported and grown. While this issue does not seem to be as prevalent within many Churches, I still feel compelled to address this issue due to the growing popularity within churches of government sponsored welfare programs. To examine how the Church should respond to welfare programs, we must first consider what the Bible says about the issue. The following verses speak directly about acts of charity, and should therefore form the basis of the response of the Church to this societal issue.

- Isaiah 58:10 reads, "Feed the hungry, and help those in trouble. Then your light will

- shine out from the darkness, and the darkness around you will be as bright as noon."

- Acts 20:35 says, "And I have been a constant example of how you can help those in need by working hard. You should remember the words of the Lord Jesus: It is more blessed to give than to receive."

- Luke 12:33 reads, "Sell your possessions, and give to the needy. Provide yourselves with moneybags that do not grow old, with a treasure in the heavens that does not fail, where no thief approaches and no moth destroys."

Considering these verses, I do not believe it is possible to hold a Biblical worldview and believe that it is the responsibility of the government to provide welfare programs, rather than the Church and the individual

Christian. While it is true the

Israelites are commanded in the Torah

(what Christians know as the Old

Testament) to give charitably both

individually and through the State, I

believe it is important to note that

Israel was, and largely remains, what

we now consider a theocracy. The

Isrealite nation, when it was not

acting out in sin, was largely

dominated by the Levites and

prophets. Additionally, Jesus placed

many responsibilities formerly given

to the Levites on the individual. For

example, Christians no longer need a

priest to intercede with God on our

behalf- we can directly speak to God

by ourselves. I believe the shift from

the church to the individual on many

concepts in the New Testament

includes giving charitably, though I

realize many pastors disagree with my

take-away on this issue since, to my

understanding, Jesus never refuted the

aspect of Israelite law outlining state

welfare programs.

Veganism

As with government sponsored welfare programs, this issue seems to be more relegated to the realm of social media, however the issue of veganism and calls for Christians to stop consuming meat and meat products (such as eggs and milk) are growing within many Christian circles. To examine how the Church should respond to veganism, we must first consider what the Bible says about the issue. The following verses speak directly about which foods Christians are permitted by God to consume, and should therefore form the basis of the response of the Church to this societal issue.

- Genesis 9:3 reads, "Every moving thing that lives shall be food for you. And as I gave you the green plants, I give you everything."

- 1 Timothy 4:1-4 says, "Now the Spirit expressly says that in later times some will depart from the faith by devoting themselves to deceitful spirits and teachings of demons, through the insincerity of liars whose consciences are seared, who forbid marriage and require abstinence from foods that God created to be received with thanksgiving by those who believe and know the truth. For everything created by God is good, and nothing is to be rejected if it is received with thanksgiving,"

- Romans 14:2 reads, "One person believes he may eat anything, while the weak person eats only vegetables."

- Matthew 14:19 says, "And he directed the people to sit down on the grass. Taking the five loaves and the two fish and looking up to heaven, he gave

thanks and broke the loaves.
Then he gave them to the
disciples, and the disciples gave
them to the people."

- John 21:9-12 reads, "When
they landed, they saw a fire of
burning coals there with fish on
it, and some bread. Jesus said to
them, "Bring some of the fish
you have just caught." So
Simon Peter climbed back into
the boat and dragged the net
ashore. It was full of large fish,

153, but even with so many the net was not torn. Jesus said to them, "Come and have breakfast." None of the disciples dared ask him, "Who are you?" They knew it was the Lord."

Considering these verses, I do not believe it is possible to hold a Biblical worldview and believe it is sinful or unGodly to eat meat and other meat products (such as eggs).

Globalism

Many churches, denominations, and clerical leaders have openly decried President Donald Trump's "America First" policies and advocated for globalism. Some churches even equate globalism with the Church itself. To examine how the Church should respond to globalism and the idea of national sovereignty, we must first consider what the Bible says about the issue. The following verses speak directly about national

sovereignty, and should therefore

form the basis of the response of the

Church to this societal issue.

- Romans 13:1 reads, "Let

  everyone be subject to the

  governing authorities, for there

  is no authority except that

  which God has established. The

  authorities that exist have been

  established by God."

- 1 Peter 2:13-17 says, "Be subject for the Lord's sake to every human institution, whether it be to the emperor as supreme, or to governors as sent by him to punish those who do evil and to praise those who do good. For this is the will of God, that by doing good you should put to silence the ignorance of foolish people. Live as people who are free, not using your freedom as a cover-up for evil, but living as servants of God. Honor everyone. Love the brotherhood. Fear God. Honor the emperor."

- Matthew 22:21b reads, "Then he said to them, "Therefore render to Caesar the things that are Caesar's, and to God the things that are God's."

- Daniel 2:21 says, "He changes times and seasons; he removes kings and sets up kings; he gives wisdom to the wise and

knowledge to those who have

understanding;"

- Isaiah 9:6 reads, "For to us a

  child is born, to us a son is

  given; and the government shall

  be upon his shoulder, and his

  name shall be called Wonderful

  Counselor, Mighty God,

  Everlasting Father, Prince of

  Peace."

- Deuteronomy 16:18-20 says,

  "You shall appoint judges and

officers in all your towns that

the Lord your God is giving

you, according to your tribes,

and they shall judge the people

with righteous judgment. You

shall not pervert justice. You

shall not show partiality, and

you shall not accept a bribe, for

a bribe blinds the eyes of the

wise and subverts the cause of

the righteous. Justice, and only

justice, you shall follow, that

you may live and inherit the

land that the Lord your God is

giving you."

Considering these verses, I

believe one holding a Biblical

worldview must believe nations are

established by God and governments

derive their authority from God.

Therefore, I do not believe the idea of

Globalism to be Biblical, and, though

I did not include the particular verse

due to it's inevitability, I believe

Christians are warned of Globalism as

a sign of the end times.

Border Wall

Since becoming elected as President of the United States in November of 2016, Donald Trump has increasingly called for, and even begun construction of, a border wall along the Southern border of the United States to help fight illegal immigration. As a result, many within the Church have vocally decried President Trump's immigration policies and have advocated globalism. To examine how the Church should respond to President Trump's push to create a wall along the Southern border of the United States, we must first consider what the Bible says about the issue. The following verses speak directly about nations building walls, and should therefore form the basis of the response of the Church to this societal issue.

- 2 Chronicles 14:7 reads, "For he said to Judah, "Let us build these cities and surround them with walls and towers, gates and bars. The land is still ours because we have sought the Lord our God; we have sought Him, and He has given us rest on every side." So they built and prospered."

- Nehemiah 2:17 says, "Then I said to them, "You see the bad situation we are in, that

Jerusalem is desolate and its gates burned by fire. Come, let us rebuild the wall of Jerusalem so that we will no longer be a reproach."

- Proverbs 25:28 reads, "Like a city that is broken into and without walls Is a man who has no control over his spirit."

Considering these verses, I believe it is not possible to hold a Biblical worldview and oppose the creation of a wall dividing national

borders.

Immigration

The issue of immigration has been a "hot-button topic" within the United States for many years. Democrats have repeatedly called for completely open borders while Republicans seek to reform immigration to the United States. I did not address immigration in the globalism or border wall pages, because I believe the three issues are closely related but still separate. To examine how the Church should respond to immigration, we must first consider what the Bible says about the issue. The following verses speak directly about how a nation should treat immigrants to their land.

- Leviticus 19:33-34 reads, "When a stranger sojourns with you in your land, you shall not do him wrong. You shall treat the stranger who sojourns with you as the native among you, and you shall love him as yourself, for you were strangers in the land of Egypt: I am the Lord your God."

- Exodus 22:21 says, ""You shall not wrong a sojourner or oppress him, for you were sojourners in the land of Egypt."

- Exodus 23:9 reads, ""You shall not oppress a sojourner. You know the heart of a sojourner, for you were sojourners in the land of Egypt."

- Deuteronomy 27:19 says, "'Cursed be anyone who perverts the justice due to the sojourner, the fatherless, and the widow.' And all the people shall say, 'Amen.'

- Romans 13:1-7 reads, "Let every person be subject to the governing authorities. For there is no authority except from

God, and those that exist have been instituted by God."

- Exodus 12:49 says, "There shall be one law for the native and for the stranger who sojourns among you."

- Deuteronomy 10:19 reads, "Love the sojourner, therefore, for you were sojourners in the land of Egypt."

- Leviticus 24:22 says, "You shall have the same rule for the sojourner and for the native, for

I am the Lord your God."

Considering these verses, I do

not believe one can hold a Biblical

worldview and oppose legal

immigration. However, I also believe

it is made clear that immigrants are to

follow the laws of the land in which

they are living.

Islam and Other, Non-Christian Religions

Increasingly popular within worldly culture is the idea that all religions worship the same God; that somehow the God of the Bible is the same as the god of Islam (despite the stark and abundant theological contrasts between Christianity and Islam). In January of 2020, Pope Francis met with Sheikh Yahya Cholil

Staque, leader of the world's largest Muslim organization, and seemingly advanced the idea that the God of the Bible is the same as, or at least very similar to, the god of Islam. To examine how the Church should respond to the idea of a "universal god", we must first consider what the Bible says about the issue. The following verses speak directly about God's sovereignty, and the salvation offered only by Jesus.

- Exodus 23:13 reads, ""Pay attention to all that I have said to you, and make no mention of the names of other gods, nor let it be heard on your lips."

- Deuteronomy 6:14 says, "You shall not go after other gods, the gods of the peoples who are around you"

- John 14:6 reads, "Jesus said to him, "I am the way, and the truth, and the life. No one comes to the Father except through me."

- Exodus 20:1-5 reads, "And God spoke all these words, saying, "I am the Lord your God, who brought you out of the land of Egypt, out of the house of slavery. "You shall have no other gods before me. "You shall not make for yourself a carved image, or any likeness of anything that is in heaven above, or that is in the earth beneath, or that is in the water under the earth. You shall not bow down to them or serve them, for I the Lord your God am a jealous God, visiting the iniquity of the fathers on the children to the third and the fourth generation of those who hate me"

- Matthew 6:24 says, ""No one can serve two masters, for either he will hate the one and love the other, or he will be devoted to the one and despise

the other..."

Considering these verses, I do

not believe it is possible to hold a

Biblical worldview and support Islam,

Islamic policies, or any other religion

or religious principle other than

Christianity.

Race

Following the undeniably tragic death of George Floyd, racial tensions within the United States have erupted. As a result, political division is at an all-time high at the time of this paper's publishing. Many within even very traditional churches have called for white people to apologize for slavery and other historical wrongs and to also denounce "white privilege". To examine how the

Church should respond to racism, in all forms racism may rear it's ugly head, we must first consider what the Bible says about the issue. The following verses speak directly about humanity and race.

- Genesis 1:27 reads, "So God created man in his own image, in the image of God he created him; male and female he created them."

- Matthew 22:39b says, "Thou shalt love thy neighbor as thyself"

- Galatians 3:28 reads, "There is neither Jew nor Greek, there is neither slave nor free, there is no male and female, for you are all one in Christ Jesus."

- John 7:24 says, "Do not judge by appearances, but judge with right judgment."

- Acts 17:26 reads, "And he made from one man every

nation of mankind to live on all
the face of the earth, having
determined allotted periods and
the boundaries of their dwelling
place"

- John 13:34 says, "A new
commandment I give to you,
that you love one another: just
as I have loved you, you also
are to love one another."

- James 2:9 reads, "But if you
show partiality, you are
committing sin and are

convicted by the law as transgressors."

- Matthew 28:19 says, "Go therefore and make disciples of all nations, baptizing them in the name of the Father and of the Son and of the Holy Spirit,"

Considering these verses, I do not believe it is possible to hold a Biblical worldview and treat any race as superior to another, regardless of circumstances or "justifications". If

Christians are to Biblically respond to incidents of racism, regardless of who is committing it (be it white on black, black on white, or any other situation in which racism becomes the root of evil), we must respond to hate with love and treat all people equally.

Political/Social Apathy

As I myself have learned first-hand, there are many Christians, even traditional Christians, who believe a Christian should completely distance him or herself from politics. One clergyman I know even told me I needed to "keep Jesus out of politics", and another has told me "we cannot push Christian ideals in our secular society, because we cannot expect Atheists and other non-Christians to live certain ways". To examine how involved the Church should be involved in politics and advocate for Biblical ideals, we must first consider what the Bible says about the issue, and as Americans, we need to also consider the thoughts of our Founding Fathers on the subject. The following Bible verses and quotes from our Founding Fathers speak directly about Christians in government.

- Romans 13:1 reads, "Let every person be subject to the governing authorities. For there is no authority except from God, and those that exist have been instituted by God."

- 1 Timothy 2:1-2 says, "First of all, then, I urge that supplications, prayers, intercessions, and thanksgivings be made for all people, for kings and all who are in high positions, that we may lead a peaceful and quiet life, godly and dignified in every way."

- Matthew 22:17-21 reads, "Tell us, then, what you think. Is it lawful to pay taxes to Caesar, or not?" But Jesus, aware of their malice, said, "Why put me to the test, you hypocrites? Show me the coin for the tax." And they brought him a denarius. And Jesus said to them, "Whose likeness and inscription is this?" They said,

"Caesar's." Then he said to

them, "Therefore render to

Caesar the things that are

Caesar's, and to God the things

that are God's."

- Psalm 33:12 says, "Blessed is

the nation whose God is the

Lord, the people whom he has

chosen as his heritage!"

- Acts 5:29 reads, "But Peter and

the apostles answered, "We

must obey God rather than men."

- Matthew 28:18 says, "And Jesus came and said to them, "All authority in heaven and on earth has been given to me."

- Daniel 2:21 reads, "He changes times and seasons; he removes kings and sets up kings; he gives wisdom to the wise and knowledge to those who have understanding;"

- Proverbs 14:34 says,

  "Righteousness exalts a nation,

  but sin is a reproach to any

  people."

- Proverbs 29:2 reads, "When the

  righteous increase, the people

  rejoice, but when the wicked

  rule, the people groan."

- 2 Chronicles 7:14 reads, "If my

  people who are called by my

  name humble themselves, and

  pray and seek my face and turn

  from their wicked ways, then I

will hear from heaven and will forgive their sin and heal their land."

- Genesis 19:13b says, "The outcry to the Lord against its people is so great that he has sent us to destroy it."

- Matthew 4:19 reads, "Come, follow Me," Jesus said, "and I will make you fishers of men."

- "Only a virtuous people are capable of freedom". (Benjamin Franklin)

- "The general principles on which the fathers achieved independence were the general principles of Christianity. I will avow that I then believed, and now believe, that those general principles of Christianity are as eternal and immutable as the existence and attributes of God" (John Adams)

- "The hope of a Christian is inseparable from his faith. Whoever believes in the Divine inspiration of the Holy Scriptures must hope that the religion of Jesus shall prevail throughout the earth. Never since the foundation of the world have the prospects of mankind been more encouraging to that hope than they appear to be at the present time. And may the associated distribution of the Bible proceed and prosper till the Lord shall have made "bare His holy arm in the eyes of all the nations, and all the ends of the earth shall see the salvation of our God" [Isaiah 52:10]" (John Quincy Adams)

- In 1854, Congress adopted a resolution which reads, in part, "The great, vital, and conservative element in our system is the belief of our people in the pure doctrines and the divine truths of the Gospel of Jesus Christ"

- "Mankind, when left to themselves, are unfit for their own government" (George Washington)

- "It is impossible to rightly govern a nation without God and the Bible." (George Washington)

Considering these verses, I do not believe it is possible to hold a

Biblical worldview and be apathetic to politics and social issues. Christians cannot expect non-Christians to act in a Godly manner, but we are still called to push for Biblical ideals and to uphold the government to certain standards, because God clearly hates sins and punishes nations for acting sinfully. Because the lost are going to act in sin, does not give Christians a "pass" for the sin of the nation in which they live, especially since we have been explicitly called to engage in

evangelism and sharing the Gospel.

The burden for the state of our nation,

therefore, has been placed upon all

Christians. Considering these quotes,

I also do not believe that our

Founding Fathers intended for our

government to be secular in nature, or

that our nation's Founders intended

for God to be kept out of the

government (rather than the

government kept out of the Church).

Summary

In summary, though the intentions of the world are often good, it seems as though nearly every position worldly culture advocates for are in direct contradiction to the Bible. Many positions at first glance may even appear Godly, but the fact remains these programs run contrary to the teachings of Scripture. Furthermore, it is impossible to be a Christian without believing in the fullness and inerrancy of the Bible, otherwise one's faith will be like that of a house built upon sand-foundationless. Therefore, I do not believe it is possible for a Christian to support worldly ideals.

With all of this in mind, especially considering the cultural divide within the Church itself, it is important for all Christians to strengthen our individual Biblical worldviews, advocate what is truly Biblical, oppose the lies and manipulations of the Devil, seek to reunite many denominations with the Bible as the foundation of each denomination, and pray for our nation and the Church as a whole. As Balthasar Hubmaier once said, "Truth is Immortal".

About the Author

James King is a 2019 graduate from Georgia Baptist college Truett McConnell University, where he earned a degree in the Great Commission (Evangelism). In addition to *The Elephant in the Sanctuary*, James has written *Visions of Yonah* (a historical picture book of White County, Georgia), *Making the Case for Socialism: An Examination of the Accomplishments of Socialism* (which is meant to be a gag gift), and

Faces in these Hills (a book of local

ghost stories from White County,

Georgia). All four books are available

for purchase on Amazon in both

paperback and Kindle formats.

Currently, James serves as the

Minister of Music for a Baptist

Church in Toccoa, Georgia, is the

Chairman of Young Republicans of

Northeast Georgia, cheers on the

University of Georgia Bulldogs every

Fall, is committed to Making America

Great Again, and married the love of

his life on August 1, 2020!

www.ingramcontent.com/pod-product-compliance
Lightning Source LLC
Chambersburg PA
CBHW031237250726
48655CB00005B/2001